Praise for *TERROR COUNTER*

"Anyone who understands poetry as a search for liberation, whatever the level of that liberation, will hold *TERROR COUNTER* as compass. Filled with fierce lyric tenderness and clear-eyed commitment to revolutionary aesthetic, *TERROR COUNTER* is devoted to the redemption of the self from a world ready to usurp this resistance. Fargo Nissim Tbakhi is a Palestinian poetic being of the most natural order. Just wait until you arrive at his elegy for his father. If you're lucky, you will understand what Sirhan Sirhan means. If you're lucky, Tbakhi's performance will let you taste what free is."

—Fady Joudah, author of *[...]*

"To tunnel through land is to become a root. To tunnel through language is to become its song. Fargo Nissim Tbakhi's poetry does both, is both—the faithful becoming of the heartbeat. Because *TERROR COUNTER* is a fight to the LIFE! It is a fight against the state, the black site of American literature, the empire of possibilityeaters. It is a fight to undo being, to be for others, for all. And it is a fight for the right to dream of a future, the future, that is Palestine. Liberation is love poetry. Bring your heart, dear reader. Bring your crowbar."

—Brandon Shimoda, author of *The Grave on the Wall*

"In this debut collection electric with grief, rage, and love, Tbakhi enacts the liberatory possibilities of a language reclaimed. Through a variety of invented forms and stirring unravelings, these poems tunnel, excavate, eulogize, exclaim, and most elegantly imagine where we might go once we reject the dehumanizing gaze and obsessions of a crumbling empire and return to ourselves and to each other. This book will crack your heart open. Let it, let the light come pouring in."

—Lena Khalaf Tuffaha, author of *Something About Living*

Terror Counter

Fargo Nissim Tbakhi

DEEP VELLUM PUBLISHING

DALLAS, TEXAS

Deep Vellum Publishing
3000 Commerce St., Dallas, Texas 75226
deepvellum.org · @deepvellum

Deep Vellum is a 501c3 nonprofit literary arts organization
founded in 2013 with the mission to bring
the world into conversation through literature.

Copyright © 2025 Fargo Nissim Tbhaki

First edition, 2025
All rights reserved.

Support for this publication has been provided in part by grants from the National Endowment for the Arts, the Texas Commission on the Arts, the City of Dallas Office of Arts and Culture, the Communities Foundation of Texas, and the Addy Foundation.

This work of poetry is presented as part of the Central Track Poetry Series, a collaboration between Deep Vellum and SMU's Project Poëtica.

ISBNs: 978-1-64605-379-7 (paperback) | 978-1-64605-392-6 (ebook)

LIBRARY OF CONGRESS CATALOGING-IN-PUBLICATION DATA

Names: Tbakhi, Fargo Nissim, author.
Title: Terror counter / Fargo Nissim Tbakhi.
Other titles: Terror counter (Compilation)
Description: First English edition. | Dallas, Texas : Deep Vellum Publishing, 2025.
Identifiers: LCCN 2024059397 (print) | LCCN 2024059398 (ebook) | ISBN 9781646053797 (trade paperback) | ISBN 9781646053926 (ebook)
Subjects: LCSH: Palestinians--Poetry. | Palestinian Americans--Poetry. | Palestine--Poetry. | LCGFT: Poetry.
Classification: LCC PS3620.B35 T47 2025 (print) | LCC PS3620.B35 (ebook) | DDC 811/.6--dc23/eng/20241218
LC record available at https://lccn.loc.gov/2024059397
LC ebook record available at https://lccn.loc.gov/2024059398

Cover © Hani Zurob 'Within Time no. 1' (2020), Charcoal and pens on canson paper, 65x50 cm
Interior Layout and Typesetting by KGT

PRINTED IN THE UNITED STATES OF AMERICA

For Palestinians, those who love us, and those we love.
Against the world.

In furtherance of the conspiracy, and to carry out its objects, the following overt acts, among others, were committed
   —USA v Abaji et al., U.S. District Court for the Central District of California

CONTENTS

Terror Counter   3

IMPERIAL POETICS LTD
Of   7
An American Writes a Poem   8
Spiders   10
For Sami Abu Diak   12
Palestinian Love Poem   14
Olive Tree Pastoral   15
Olive Tree Necropastoral   16
The Dream of the Anti-Ekphrasis   17
Exchange Value   19
Palestinian Love Poem   20
Parable   21
Poetry   23
Craft Talk   24
Song of Naming   26

Terror Counter   28

GAZAN TUNNELS
Through the Defence (Emergency) Regulations   31
Through Yehuda Amichai's "Sonnet"   32
Through the Balfour Declaration   33
Through the Defence (Emergency) Regulations   34
Through Basic Law: Israel as the Nation State of the Jewish People   35
Through Remarks by President Biden on the Middle East   36
Through the Defence (Emergency) Regulations   37
Through USA v Abaji et al.   38
Through the Defence (Emergency) Regulations   42

Terror Counter   45

PALESTINE IS A FUTURISM
PALESTINE IS A FUTURISM   49

Terror Counter   66

RITHA' AL NAFS

Passing Season	71
Incantation	76
Songs of Unnaming	78
Prayer	82
In the Knowledge that You Will Die, and I Will Die	83
Terror Counter	97
Notes & Acknowledgments	99

TERROR COUNTER

Terror Counter

everything is extricable.

nothing is extant.

we are an i. we are a door.

we are locked.

all our means of relation disappear into the grind.

the grind is he who slicks my oil throat.

*i am hijacking every thing.
watch: I. I. I. I. I. I. I. I. I. I. I.
I. I. I. I. I. I. I. I. I. I. I. I. I. I. I.
I. I. I. I. I. I. I. I. I. I. I. I. I. I. I.*

*the feeling of fear is a good one.
half-shaped, we tumble from the
politic's mouth. the giant picks
us up, peers at our oilskins, our
yesterday muscles. the giant
returns us to the grind. dandruff
speckles from my skull and each
fleck is a drone, warning the
bathers of a shark which cannot
end and does not stop. what it is
to count the state of our forever.
to receive a grant for the way
my beard does or does not
engender fear, my handful of
dust. to regulate the fingers of
each pore, the language of my
wildness. the blood flowing like
a trade caravan. i am invaded
by blood which wields a razor,
which tames my wildness. i am*

       hairless now, smooth as a
                    baby's
                     neck.
a baby's neck. a baby. a baby. a
       baby's neck. a baby wailing
   forever. interred in rock. soot. a
    baby's fingernails, too small to
   offer protection to any power.
   inside the poem trapped. frozen
      into submission. transfers of
       meaning. terror and light.
   cemeteries of courts. bled for a
       dollar. my page count of
    sorrow. ironically poisoned no
     honesty left. songs inside letters
    hands inside wells. the wail of it
     a path i seek to follow. the wail
     of it singing: I. I. I. I. I. I. I. I.
   I. I. I. I. I. I. I. I. I. I. I. I. I. I. I.
    I. I. I. I. I. I. I. I. I. I. I. I. I. I.
                I. I. I. I. I need

IMPERIAL POETICS LTD

They dip their pens in our hearts and think they are inspired.
—Kahlil Gibran, *Sand and Foam*

IMPERIAL POETICS BID

Of

After Milton, for George

my last obedience to the restraints Of the language Of bone breakers,
to the tyranny inside the gloved hand, inside Of, I dissolve it now,
I offer it to you slaughtered like a purveyor Of tear gas, gutted like
a sustainer Of museums, I beg you now, who from the last
will be present, anchoring my every tooth, planted in a garden
fertilized by the ashes Of Qalandia, rend my body, bring life to Arabs,
bring water to wash my body Of blood, I will be wrath Of,
song Of, blade and flame Of, tooth and nail Of, I will entomb
the remnants Of a board Of directors inside my own heart,
your hands forgiving the debts Of rule, translating the missives
Of scorpions, the homilies Of Molotovs, breathing the desiccations
Of security cameras, you crater Of tongue, you loveliness in retribution,
tributary Of unpriced goods, Of fire and ice, Of a program to liberate,
Of the drowning of conquerors, Of an endless intifada, you singer Of
a stone to the skull Of a soldier, here I beg you with libations Of tanks,
with offerings Of hair, Of loss, Of the suit Of a banker, Of boots pried
from the feet which carried a corpse to its nest at Qalandia, I give you
my fears and my hesitancies, to cast into the depths, to unlanguage, I beg you,
lower me my heart the hewn signature Of a stonemason,
bring me low, unmake me roughly silica dust outlining my shape
like an angel silent in the poisoned air, steady my rifle
aimed toward the killing Of treeplanters, the righting Of sins,
the breathing Of earth, the dreaming Of children, Of this, Of more,
sing, empty the earth Of song to pour into my ventricled weapon,
you made with earth and a million stomping feet, what is low
in me make sharp, what is hurt in me make sharper,
and what is light in me, and what in me
is light?

An American Writes a Poem,

sells it to a university magazine run by exploited graduate students.
A different American sees the poem online
and buys the magazine for $22.95. Of this a small percentage
to the university, little to nothing to the graduate students, whose union
is fomenting daily, and with the certainty of mold.

The university courts an endowment from a conservative billionaire.
Certainly says the billionaire and drafts a quick proposal for an endowed chair
of the study of international relations through the lens of finance. The chair will
in the next year recommend a strong legal and policy response to the growing movement
for a popular boycott of Israel, which an undergrad will be surveilled
and suspended for supporting.

The billionaire files his taxes, paying roughly .5% of his declared income.
In the night his teeth grind lightly as cruelty works through his system like moss.
He will wake with no memory of his dreams, which were Artaudian, prophetic.

The billionaire's taxes go toward the production of this year's slate of U.S.
weaponry, and are pocketed by the financiers of major capital, their defense
contracts quietly renewed. At a banquet the financiers begin to vomit,
the shellfish revolting.

A percentage of this weaponry is bundled into an $800 million arms deal
with the state of Israel. A new kind of infringement on life is dreamt up,
written down, and revised, to be voted on summarily.

The arms deal pays for the restocking of an arsenal depleted
during the last escalation of genocide. The arsenal receives a fresh supply:
some 10,000 M16A1 rifles, 350 M203 grenade launchers, 200 M2 .50 caliber
machine guns, and an assortment of .30 caliber, .50 caliber,
and 20mm ammunition, among others whose names have been redacted by the linguists.

These weapons are dispersed among the various branches of Israel's occupying forces,
who are as a matter of citizenship required to take part in the military front
of the genocide. A routine settler, once they have fulfilled this requirement,
begins to serve on one of the other fronts: ideological, academic, cultural,
culinary, linguistic, political, social, economic, and the front of the dreaming.

One of the soldiers, issued a rifle which fires black sponge rounds,
introduced in 2015, heavier and thus more lethal than typical sponge-tipped rounds,
which are classified by the occupation forces as nonlethal
despite evidence to the contrary,
clambers into his AIL Storm border police Jeep
produced by Automotive Industries Ltd on a Chrysler license,
and scrolls on his phone as the Jeep rumbles toward Al-Ram.

He sees the poem. He reads its lines to himself silently.
They enact something about grief, in his first language. He thinks
about Brooklyn. He screenshots the poem before clambering
out of the Jeep to aim at the youths throwing stones,
most of which are likely repurposed rubble from bombed buildings
previously understood by some to be homes.

Irritated, the soldier fires a black sponge round into a child's chest,
which causes massive internal bleeding that will later cause the child,
my cousin Muhyee, to die.

This is the place analysis ends.

The soldier will go home and surrender to the dream of militant preservation.
He will never think of this day again.

I will think of this day constantly.
Imagining and reimagining the round
hurtling through the wind, as again an American poem
just breaks somebody's heart

Spiders
for Jess

Three times in three days I turned my eyes to see
a spider at the moment it caught and ate a fly.
I wake wrapped in dread next to a father who's died.
He's not wrapped in anything. My dream of creaturely fact.
Cook flour and water and you can make flesh.
My puppet wrapped in distance and law. I wake
wrapped in capital. A spider hid the prophet and kept him
safe from harm. How to be lucky
in the time of time and nothing but time meted out variously.
A child in my grandmother's house my friend the spider.
My daddy long legs who could kill me but couldn't.
I wish for everybody fullness. Let me have a leg inside every world.
To see what could cause me to die and to watch it not
move. I used to whisper to trees and then I stopped. Then, later,
I saw a very small spider next to a very large scorpion, both
dead. Today is my father's birthday. I have not seen a spider eat
for several weeks. Outside my window several spiders a kinship of them
sharing one web. From them I learn violence, homemaking.
Jess tells me there's a metaphor scuttling across her ceiling and that spiders
are not my friends. I'm trying to write a review of the terrible book
about Palestine but I can't. I watched a gust of wind blow
and uproot a bush in the neighbor's bougie yard on the day I wished
this country would end. I know the world has agency.
Wealth makes people evil and so boring I want to puke.
The spiders live in all the corners of the house the places things meet.
The terrible poetry book about Palestine keeps calling everything we do
a poem, my dad is a poem, our scars are poems, annexation is a poem,
the land is a poem, etc. I won't do that to spiders they're not poems
they're creatures and they know things. I've been hungry and eaten.
I've been eaten too. I've been practicing flying. I'm starting to find the words I need.
I'm starting to know they'll never work. I don't have teeth
to speak of. And Jess tells me that hope and faith are different.

My dad's starting to disappear and I'm praying him along. I want
to bless him with the joy of not being known endlessly. I want to wrap
him. The wealth of the writer of the terrible book about Palestine
grows, makes nothing happen. Of the spiderearth I ask: cocoon me in wind.
Uproot me. Bite me and get past this skin, my aegis.
I don't know why anyone writes poems that aren't spells.
Most things are performative I'd say. I've got maybe seventy dollars
to my name. Performative doesn't mean fake. I think faith is knowing
there's a better world and hope is the moments it breaks
through into this one. Like a fang piercing my skin. Like one of
the strings breaking and puppet flesh spilling out into realness. I don't know
how to fly. I'm stuck weblike. The earth tells me something
about faith every single moment of every day.
Anyone with wealth is incapable of listening and they are so full of blood.
I haven't seen a spider eat since that week I wished
this country would die. Be drained.
Since then I haven't seen a spider try to teach me: nourishment
means some body needs to get exsanguinated.

For Sami Abu Diak
and every prisoner

The first time I weep for you my skin splits—here, and here, two bumps of flesh birthing bone. I had never considered antlers, though immolation crossed my mind. Blood rivers down from my mortartube wounds and paints me tatreez patterned. Each time I weep again for you, my antlers grow longer and sprout new comrades. Within a day they have reached the ocean. While I continue to weep until my forehead longs to split again, squid trace my antlers with their tentacles; they are looking for the way home. Moving along with my antlers, the squid interrupt a coast guard's ship patrolling the blurred end of international waters, wrap themselves around the enforcers and begin to squeeze. I cannot see, remaining as I am in my easy chair, but my antlers tell me that the deaths were painful. Mean time my antlers have reached the Mediterranean. Today, it is dry. Along its floor long-repressed creatures skulk, scowling at their first sun. When the scientists come from the neighboring Nations, with scopes, the floorcreatures make short work of them. I have been weeping and growing my antlers while I have been going about my days: shopping for groceries, selling my last organ to buy groceries, buying in to an idea of time that will use me up and use me up and let me waste. And every time I see or hear or speak a letter of the alphabet, or breathe, or instruct my muscles to motion, I weep for you. Every time I weep for you my antlers grow, and grow, each a vein pulsing with the rush of my own blood. They grow back onto the coast and beyond. I am at this point unable to move for the weight of them. Until, finally, they stop, though I weep ceaseless. Until, finally, it takes only the smallest twitch of my head to jut them upward into your Prison guard's two lungs, depriving It at last the privilege of breath. The Prison guard dies and no one motions a muscle to stop It from dying. I stop weeping and cry. My antlers split and enter every keyhole and burst them open like pomegranates. And all of us weep ourselves antler enough to do the same tomorrow. My weapons, goring a path to die in my father's two arms.

Palestinian Love Poem

>Something in me wishes for a dead cell
tower.
I'm a little grime. I'm arterial clogging.
Blister
on the tongue on skin You weren't aware
could
blister. I puked up a drone today
warm
and stillbreathing. Necrosis of the giver
give
to all the grimes a gift: cleanness.
Up
the throat and toward fresh air. My
goodness
what a pretty taste. The interrogatory lawyer
bends
me over and his briefcase touches my
soul.
I'm a little filth. Blood of a good man
catch
it in my cupped hands. To drink You is to
know
who I will become. I'm a little pest.
Warbling
my little deathsong like a king's
bane.
I swear I can see through myself tonight,
all
the way through to You, my watcher, my
sweet
interlocutor, silently workshopping
all
of my lines.

Olive Tree Pastoral

"They mean something,
these family gnarls, twisted
angels. Each branch might be
a lesson in history, that object
of weight and recourse. Each
olive a divine spirit of a young
boy, hurling a stone, hurled away
himself, from a nation too heavy
to hold him up. The roots of the olive tree
grow deep, stronger than any metal, holding
all of us to the land with them. Oh, leaves
of mercy, great brown guardians of the field,
shading the hills where our forefathers
sweat, where our foremothers baked
bread to feed a people, oh little spheres,
worlds pulped down to oil which coated
a young woman's throat, so she might yell
a chant so angry she burst
into bloom,"

I recite to the American art curator. She holds my hands, her eyes solemn, wet with wonder and pity. "Yes," she says, "beautiful, so beautiful. Thank you for your words." She will now go home and forget about me, until I email to remind her to send in the recommendation letter for the grant to which I'm applying, which I will not get, but will be honored to be a finalist for. I walk out of her gallery, clutching my poems to my chest, stepping on concrete and passing a grove that I don't look at, and that doesn't look at me.

Olive Tree Necropastoral

```
They mean something                            (they ate my good lung)
rotten. I watched                              (their bark is ghost skin)
their roots slurp
my brother's viscera
like tired horses                              (my mother's skin)
and they grew tall
and I saw great mis
s    h              a
pe              (rilous their cemetery stench)
n
lumps blossom on
the trunks of them
and out hatched
drones and all of              (like unmarked graves)
them knew me
and called me             (i stumble into their collected dead)
by my chosen
name and when
they did it I was
emptied of flesh                        (soldiers piss on my leaf hair)
and the soil reached       (when they burn i stink like
at me with claws
of grass to pull
its way inside
my skin and walk
at last                                              (burning)
```

The Dream of the Anti-Ekphrasis
Three Palestinian Boys, Marwan, 1970

Death is no equalizer
Nothing is equal in the eyes of—
In the gaze of—
In the Of

Where is the third beloved head
(It is where all of our heads go)
While they stand consequential as passports
(I have hurt myself within the borders of the page)
(I have done this so they may see me)

Where are their legs their feet
(Where the soil ends and the dream begins)
I have painted myself green and mottled
I have asked my body to crumple and rupture
In the desire pulling my eyes to the paint they remain
Unreachable unreached and unreaching they remain
Where do they belong?
(Never in the marketplace of nations)
(Never in the deleterious exchange of hands)
(Never in my pitiful abject sight)
(Never in my soft abject palms)
The torsos joined into a picket line
Fused like butter in the crumpled building's dead refrigerator

Where am I to look at them this way
As though lying down for them
(Prostrate in the tall grass waiting to be discovered)
And my hands so pitiful and empty
The language of survival cold within my teeth
Whatever I am seeking it is nowhere
And whoever I wish to be is dead

(I should kiss each of their cheeks)
(I should kiss them)
(I should have kissed them)
I should not have been born

And where do they belong?
In the gentle abjection of the cactus spine a bird impaled upon it
In the blood leaking from the general's eyes as he gurgles
In the survival language cracking my teeth to flee my mouth
In the folding and crumpling of my fingers as they break
(Are broken)

Exchange Value

My relationship with my father is simple.

He lets me write about him in poems I sell for $15 each,
collected in this book I sell for a $750 advance;
I send him another $550, this month, to keep his daughters enrolled in school.

So which of us the 20 yards of cloth?
Which the coat?

So who values us?
Who keeps us warm?

Palestinian Love Poem

It is the twenty-third year of my being
uncared for, and Rush Limbaugh has died, taken
his rightful place in what Hell there may be. Tenderly
I touch my legs like an oil-slicked bird. My spirit
is sick. No sweet soil has met my lips
for months without end. What use is it to say a person
committed "war crimes?" What language breathes to catch
the hugeness of that poison? What they have committed
are unspeakable things, to be responded to with unspeech.
I gather my guts to curse and wail, I craft a claw to carve
Bush's memory from each sweet heart on earth.
Kissinger done; next Biden, Bibi, Bezos, Balfour too, I will eradicate
his lingering stench from the annals of soil
rooting my feet to my ancestors' guns. How I danced
when it was Scalia, how I laughed like a splitting of skulls.
O God of the blood-balloon, God of smoke and homemade rocket,
make me a sickle to visit each governor's home. I am sick.
My spirit is sick. I am sick with the speaking of powerful words,
I am sick with the singing of oil-slicked birds. I beg to be
broken, that I might be jagged enough to—
It is the twenty-third year
of my being alone and there are too many colonies breathing
and blinking their sorrowful eyes. And who will touch me? Who
will force my sweet jaws to split wide? Who will bless my poor
anchorless eyes, I love you—bring your crowbar, bring your heart.
Meet me at their door.

Parable

What is the value of poetry in a world so full of violence?

The question has been asked of the Wise American Poet, whose wisdom has made itself known through several volumes of verse, beloved by the many who read and reviewed them, and who is here being lauded for their most recent work which tackles the "Israel-Palestine Meaning-Failure," a term the Wise American Poet coined, as they find the term "conflict" too warlike and aggressive, and feel that it distracts from what is at the core of the issue, namely humanity. Next to the Wise American Poet on the stage, in identical chairs, are an Israeli Academic and a Palestinian Academic, there to praise the Wise American Poet and marvel at the accuracy of their line breaks.

The Israeli Academic says, *What is beautiful about this book is its objectivity.* The Palestinian Academic says nothing. The Wise American Poet nods.

The Israeli Academic says, *Wise Poet, you are able to find such beauty in such complicated, solutionless difficulties.* The Palestinian Academic says nothing. *Your words are peacebringers,* says the Israeli Academic, *they cut through the noise and bring true understanding. They are conversationcreators.* The Audience murmurs in appreciation, for they have indeed conversed with interest before the talk and will continue to do so afterward. The Palestinian Academic speaks, at last. *Back to the question at hand.*

The Audience frowns.

The Palestinian Academic adds, *If you please, O Wise One.* The Audience relaxes. The Wise American Poet nods, slowly. The Audience holds its breath. Finally, after a silence long and deep, the Wise American Poet smiles, and puts out their hands in beatification. *The sun,* they announce. *The sun shines on the Israeli as it does on the Palestinian, does it not?*

At this, the Audience erupts into applause thunderous and relieved. The Wise American Poet bows and sheds a tear, upon which the Israeli Academic, not to be outdone, weeps openly and profusely. The Palestinian Academic says nothing, and as the Audience shuffles out, pockets a modest check and leaves out the back door to avoid being spat on.

*

Tonight, the Israeli Academic sleeps soundly in their bed, gently rotting, and dreams the dream of emptiness.

The Palestinian Academic, in the tiny airport room far from sight, three hours into the interrogation, rubs their eyes and wipes a little blood from the corner of their mouth. Eventually they sleep, crammed into the hidden corner. They do not dream of poetry, but of tar.

The Wise American Poet, drinking whiskey, filing their taxes, clicks on "uncommon income" and begins to enter their royalties, smiling, dreaming the dream of Wise

American

Poetry.

Poetry

is
like
the floating
piece of silk
the spider wove
years before, carried
on the wind and now
brushing, blessing, be
-littling the spider,
who's almost all
new—a touch
of what used
to mean
home

Craft Talk

The first image, a little girl's body pulled out of the rubble,
I strike from the poem. Let her rest. Language is a failed state.

The second image my own body stripped and hung by my fingers,
less their nails, piled neatly on a nearby table, I keep.
The poem is a space to rehearse for the future.

The third image a dictum of power. Something like "the state is" or
"the Guggenheim-winning poet is." This I soften and blur.
In my weakest moments I still succumb to the desire for a book deal
and avoid threatening its keepers.

The fourth image rubble alone, pulled from the mouth of my body
hanging from a hook in the black site. This image I widen so it envelops
the entire page. Yellow bile coating the margins.
I am interested in frightening you.
I do not want to be alone anymore.

The fifth image a drone giving birth to a child with gold leaf on
its fingernails. I wipe the mucus off. I give it a name. At the edge
of the poem the baby slouches toward Jerusalem. When it crosses
the border the poem can no longer see it. The drone-child becomes
an imagined condition the poem has released into the world.
I do not know what it intends. I do not know what it will eat.

The sixth image my father, dragged into the poem against his will
once more. I suspend him here with me. I revel in our
togetherness. His nails join mine, our backs are cut, our eyes plucked out.
The cruelty of jailers infected my language.
Everything I love I turn to cruelty. The poem now is just
another cell. All I know is how to write us dead.
Inside this image I reach out my little toe

and touch the image of my father's
little toe.
The state is
crueler
than your poem
ever could be,
I make the poem
make my father say.

Song of Naming

Cactus green a lucky shade of skin.
My God, taller than a fortnight.
Holiness is where my soul resides.

I remain a solemn kind of joke.
Holistically, we pay for our breaths.
A worm is a lucky thing, unless the pigeon is.

I wonder, is my name *cool breeze*?
My God, greener than a century.
A pigeon is a lucky thing.

Wellness resides outside of language.
I beg someone to keep me whole.
I wonder, is my name   ?

My God, more beautiful than a second.
I remain a transaction of flesh for meaning.
Intelligibility being my first defeat.

I   wonder is my name
?

                              What the state does not know
                                       is going to kill it.

◆
◆
◆

Terror Counter

Subject left home approximately 4:15PM for cigarettes.
Subject portrays a willingness to die as praxis.
Subject claims belief in God.
Subject believes himself to be holy.
Subject entered poetry competition approximately 7:57PM.
Subject believes worth to be undeterminable.
Subject writes in diary "i am aching to be touched again   st [sic]."
Subject's poems entered in contest determined by review board to be threatless.
Subject is constantly legible thanks to good eyesight and healthy translations.
Subject on occasion looks into corner of room.
Subject touches himself while believing in God.
Subject is fervent.
Subject on occasion looks into mirror and whispers.
Subject left home approximately 8:16AM to visit relative.
Subject believes self to be illegible.
Subject expresses desires which might be called "unsavory" in colloquial terms, "penalizable" in others.
Subject on occasion looks into the pantry at night after praying.
After touching himself.
After writing a poem and paying a small fee to have it read by another person somewhere behind a crystal screen.
Subject is looking for God according to reading of Subject vital signs.
Subject believes himself to be for others or to be at all.
Subject on occasion looks into mirror and whispers to ask us our names.

GAZAN TUNNELS

Steal a glance at the beginning of the tunnel, and in it you will see your end.
The tunnel is another coffin.
The road leading to here is narrow, but it is not far from paradise.

—Adonis, *Concerto al-Quds*, translated by Khaled Mattawa

Through the Defence (Emergency) Regulations

"Through Yehuda Amichai's "Sonnet

Through the Balfour Declaration

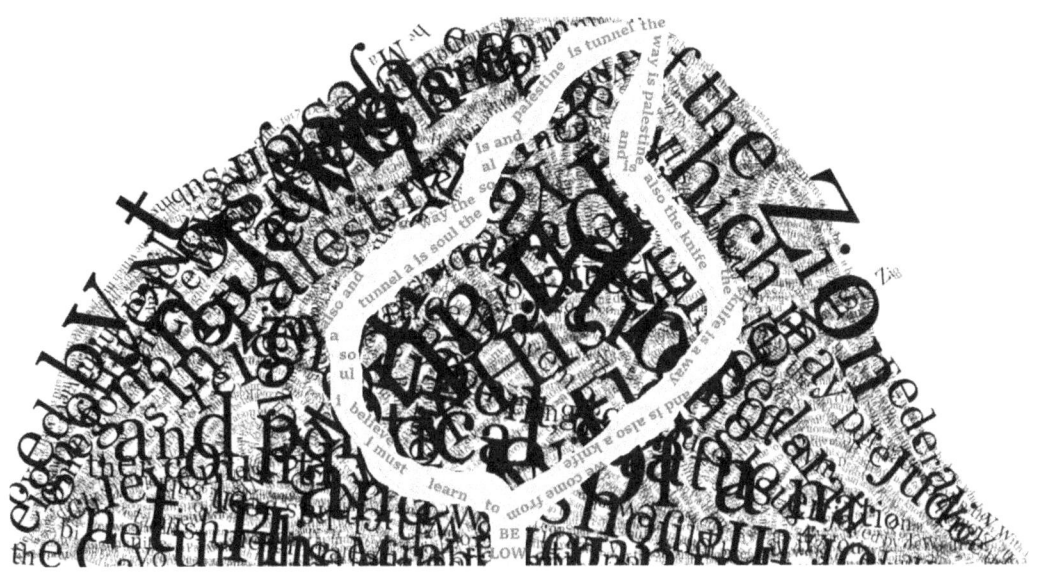

Through Defence (Emergency) Regulations

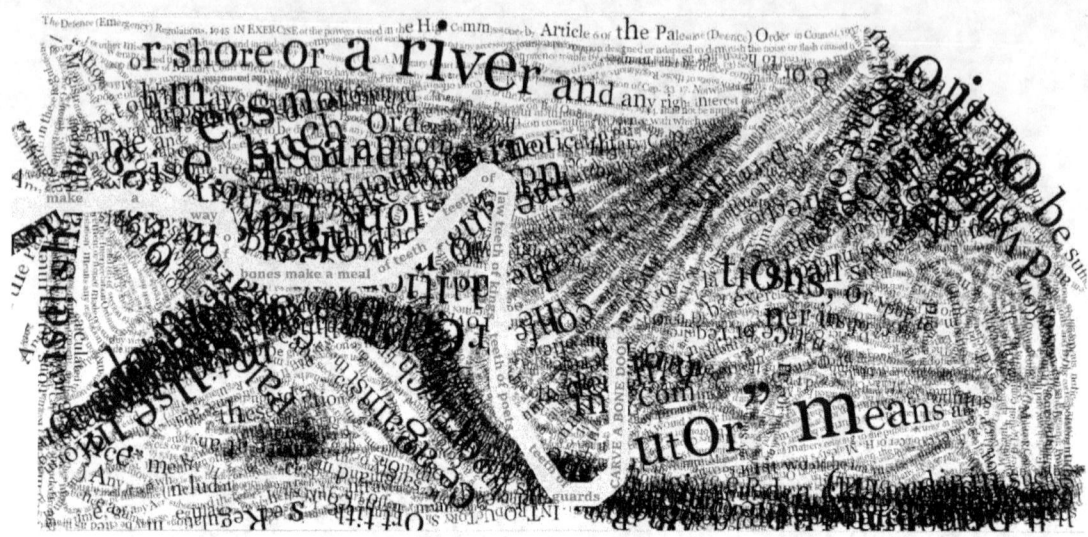

Through Basic Law: Israel as the Nation State of the Jewish People

Through Remarks by President Biden on the Middle East

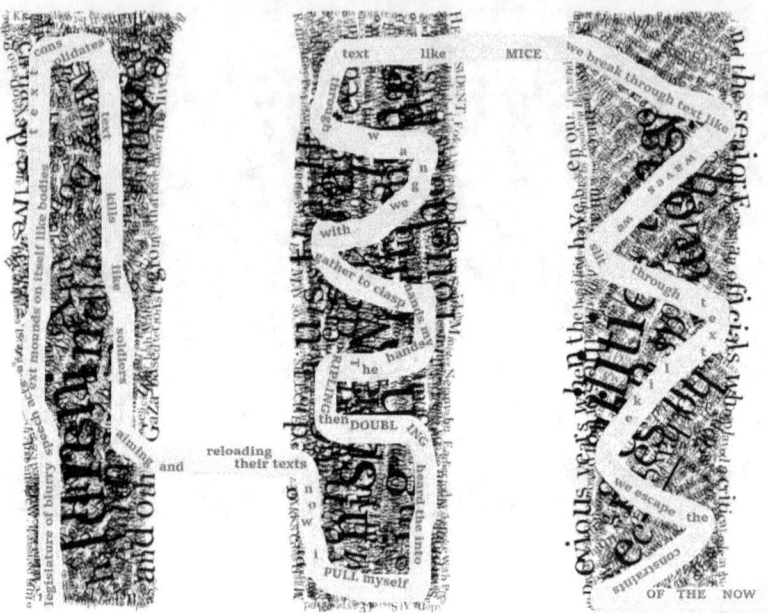

Through the Defence (Emergency) Regulations

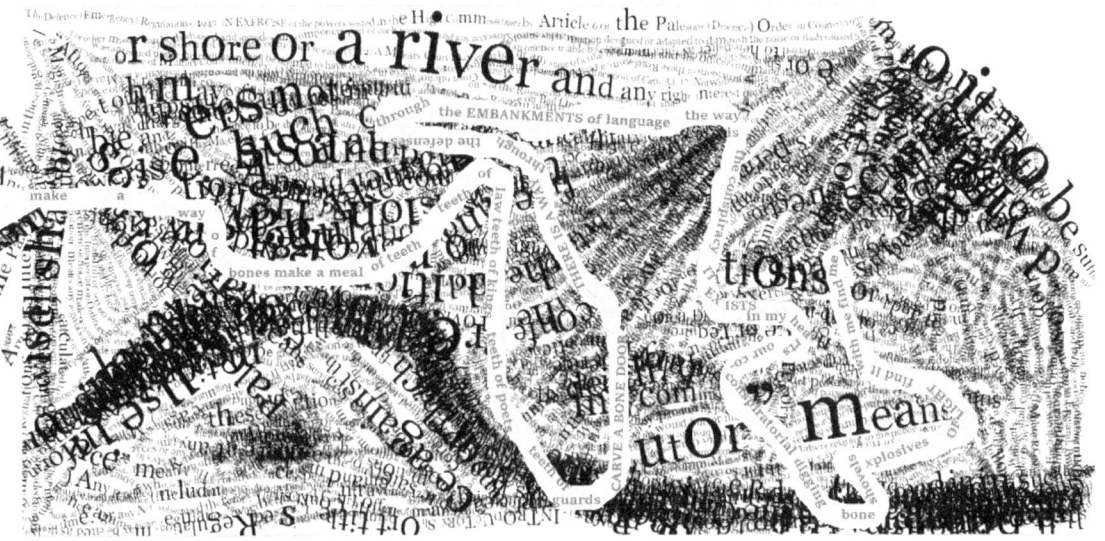

.Through USA v Abaji et al

.I

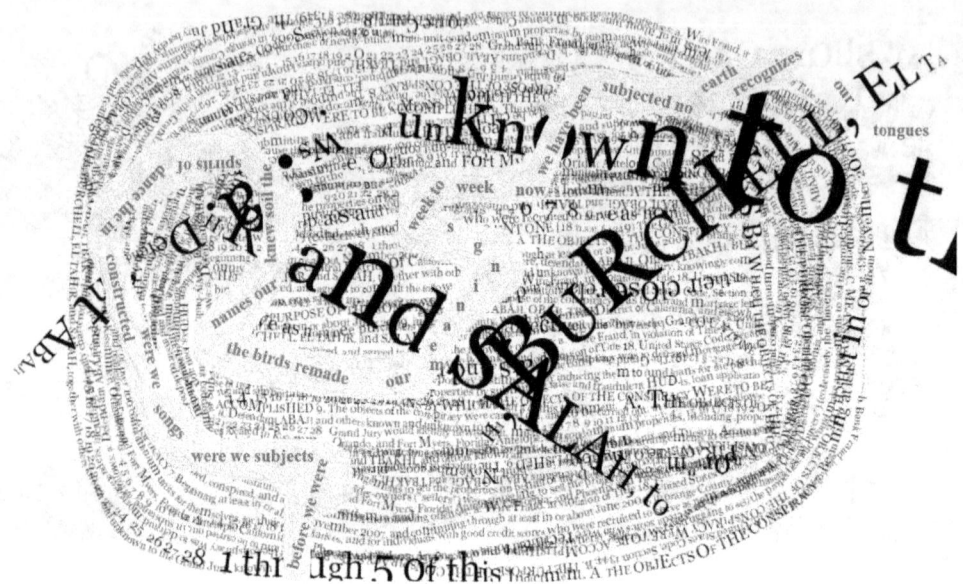

.II

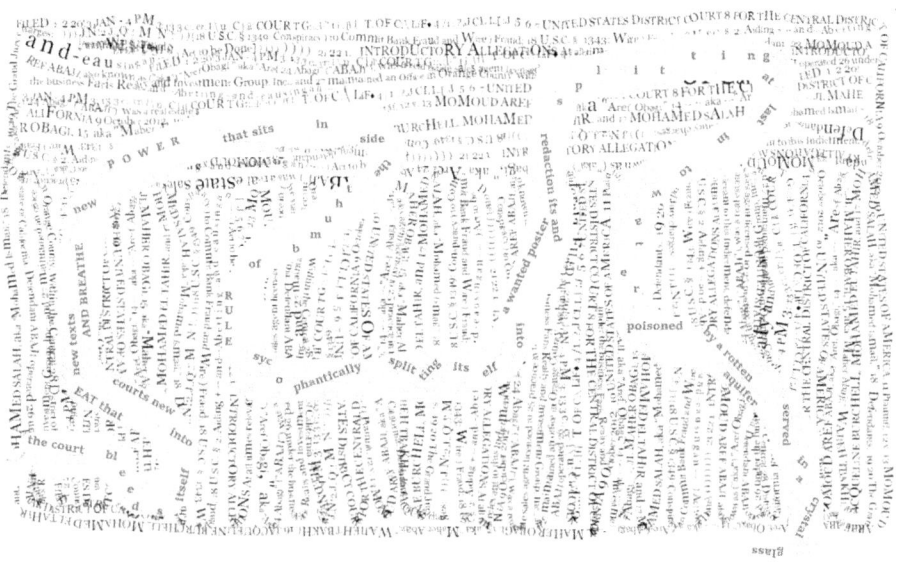

.III

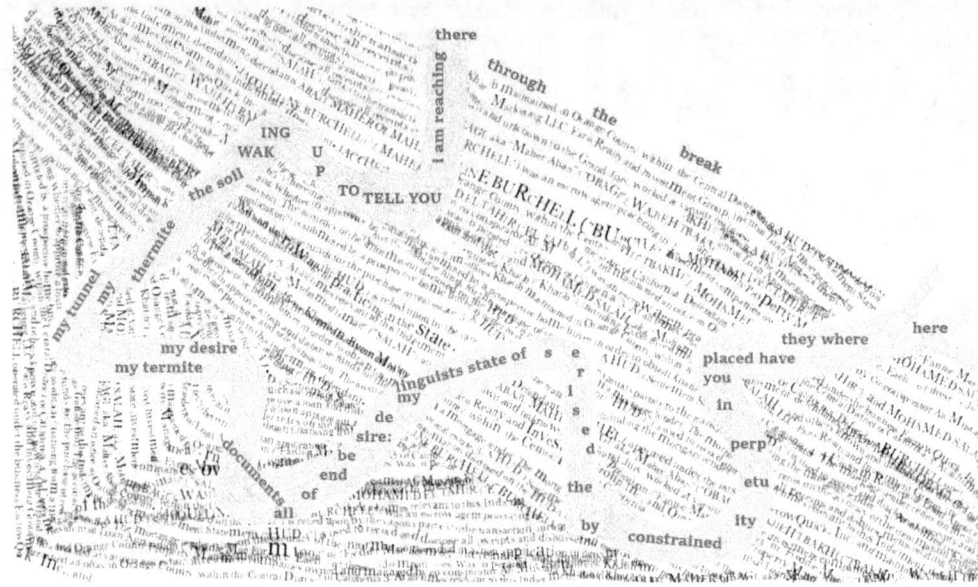

.IV

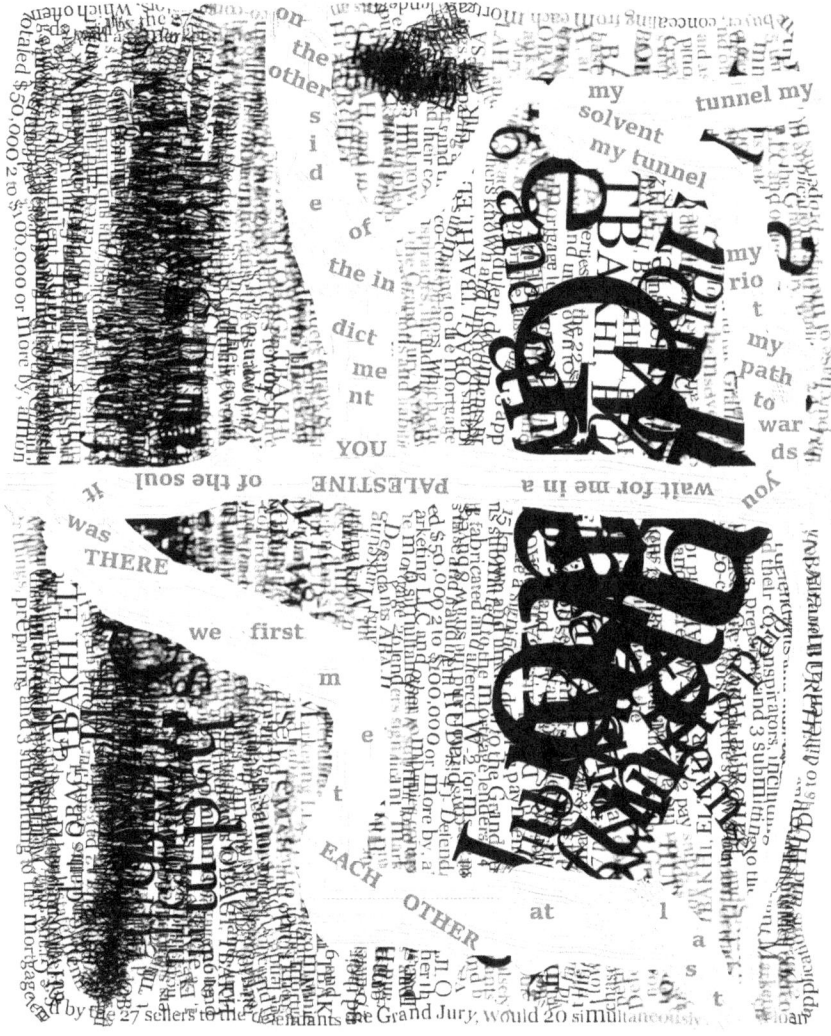

Through the Defence (Emergency) Regulations

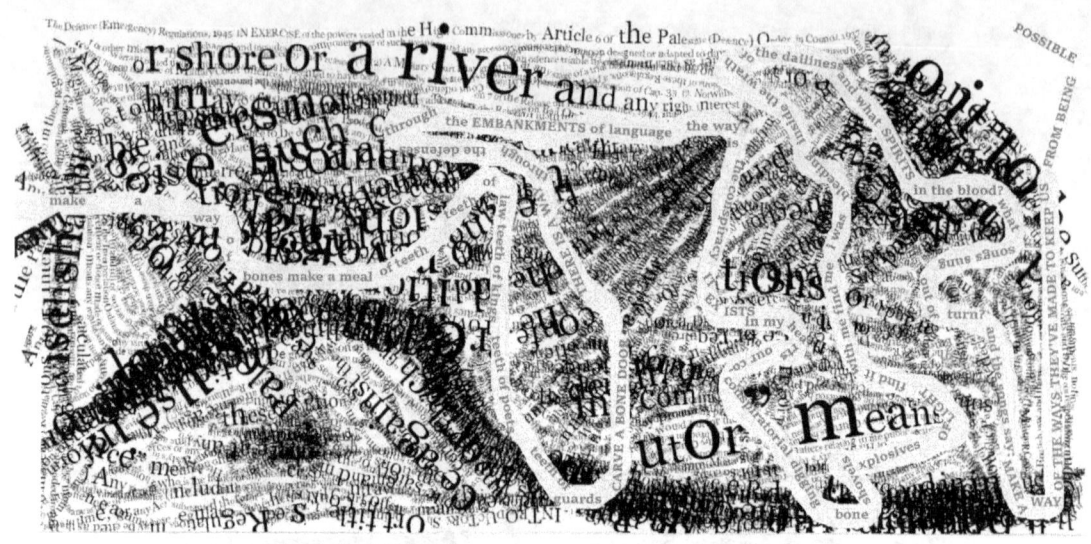

♦
♦
♦

Terror Counter

inside me every watchful eye is named and addressed i
want to breathe be dead to rights this time i want new
inventory to restock my gut there is no living outside of a
new dictionary of power we look for love and find new
masters i find my fingers have been broken in the night a
choking spirit hides within my pantry i broke them
hunger gentrifies my mouth i fold myself inside a pastry i
am broken like a sack of eggs the State has names and
addresses and arms and legs and eyes and endorphins
and epidermises and throats and teeth and tongues and
livers and mailboxes and favorite tv shows and sexual
needs and clocks and hair and guns and plastic bags and
needles and houses and spouses and fingernails and
necks and fireplaces and fetishes and books and
magazines and prizes and banks and lungs and eyebrows
and bicycles and records and pantries and condoms and
faces and faces and faces and faces and faces and faces
and faces and faces and faces and faces and faces and
faces and faces and faces and faces and faces and faces
and faces and faces and faces and faces and faces and
faces and faces and faces and faces and faces and faces
and

I   am

do You know I
am

do You know I am
somewhere
You cannot go

PALESTINE IS A FUTURISM

Our futures are in us. We are our own futures.
We will continue to know how to be Palestinian, together, when we are free. We will know better how to be Palestinian, together, as we are free.

—Sophia Azeb, "Who Will We Be When We Are Free?"

PALESTINE
IS A FUTURISM
!

WAKE WITH SUN
ENVISION SUN
HOLD SUN IN MOUTH

UNDERSTAND ALL AS SUN
SING IN HARMONY WITH WHINE OF ROCKET
SING WITH OTHERS

LEARN FORGIVENESS OF DEBTS
SING SONG OF CLASPED HANDS
BE PORTAL FOR GOD

BE VESSEL FOR SUN
NAME THE BANKS
NAME RIVER

NAME SEA
SING JOURNEY BETWEEN
BE TOOL OF LOVE

BE DREAM OF EARTH
BREATH OF SILENCE
BREATH OF GROVE

WAKE IN DEATH
HOLD DEATH
UNDO CREDIT

BE SUNTONGUE
BE DREAM OF ANTINATIONAL SONG
SLICE MELON

KISS EVERYONE
WATCH FOR SIGNS OF HEAVEN
FREE PARKING

<pre>
                FREE WINDOWS
                FREE SUNACHE
                FREE EVERYONE

            BE TUNNEL OF MERCIFUL AIR
               BE COOL BREEZE
         SING SONG OF UNDOING STRUCTURE

SING RIVER
SING SEA SING SKYWARD SING
EARTHWARD SING COUSIN
                SING OPERA

SING KNITBONE SING CARCASS SING LOVELY SING
FUNERAL
                                SING MEMORY SING GARDENER
                                    SING GLASSMAKER SING
MEMORIAL SING RETURN SING AWAKEN SING BRUTALITY
                            SING OH!

BE OPENING
BE LIGHTFINDER
BE HEAVENPATH
                BE COLONYGRINDER

                FIND A GOOD STONE
                FIND A WAY HOME

BE RIVER
                                                        BE SEA
               BE SONG OF JOURNEY BETWEEN
BE ROCKET
                      BE TUNNEL
                      BE PORCUPINE
</pre>

BE WINDOW

                    BE FISHNET
          BE SUN ALL OVER DAWNINGFREE PLACES
          AND EVERYBODY BREATHING HURRIYA!

                                                BE ALIVE
                                              STAY ALIVE
              BE RUTHLESS, FARGO

                    SURVIVE
                BEYOND SURVIVE

DIRT IS A TAUTOLOGY

WATER IS A PALLIATIVE

SLINGSHOT IS AN IDEOLOGY

CACTUS IS A MARXISM

SEA SALT IS AN INTERNATIONALISM

HUNGER IS A NEOCOLONIALISM

ELECTRICITY IS A DISPLACEMENT

ANEMONES ARE A SOLIDARITY

FISHNETS ARE A COLLECTIVISM

DIRT IS A COLLECTIVISM

MARTYRDOM IS A MATERIALISM

COUSIN IS A MATERIALISM

PALESTINE IS A FUTURISM

FUTURISM IS A PALLIATIVE

                              EMPTINESSES:
MY HEART WHEN IT IS SUFFUSED WITH ENVYPOISON

                                        LEGISLATURES

            THE SUN SHINING OUT OF OUR MOUTHS

401KS OF SALIVATING MAYORS

                  MY EYES SUFFUSED WITH THE REFLECTED DEAD

      GUTTED FISH HEAPED ON THE SIDE OF THE DOCK

                  THE TUNNEL WE DIG TO ANTITEXTUAL BLISS

501C3S OF EXPONENTIAL COMBAT VETERANS

MYTHS RENDERED IN HYPERDIMENSIONAL COLOR

THE FRIENDS I JETTISONED INTO GRAVITY'S INSISTENT RULE

                        GARROTES OF CONSULTING FIRMS

                  PEACECORPSES OF RIOTCOP THERAPISTS

            MY SOUL SUFFUSED WITH PHOSPHORESCENCE

      MY SOUL IMBUED WITH THE PEACE OF WILD MUSTARD

THE DREAM PULLS MY MEMORY FROM A WELL
I AM SERVED MEMORY FOR BREAKFAST!

                INSIDE THE DREAM I SHALL HAVE TO UNLEARN
            THE BITTERNESS OF THE WARHUNGRY CAPITALIST LIFE
              THE EMPTY MEANINGS OF THE LOBBYING FIRM!
               THE LANGUAGE THAT TURNS ME CRUEL AND USEFUL!

       IN THE DREAM I AM REQUIRED ONLY BY MY LOVERS
       NEVER THE EXTRACTIVE DRILLS OF THE OILEATERS!
         I HAVE BEEN UNMADE BY THE DREAM OF GOD
          I HAVE BEEN RELEASED FROM MEANING!

THE SUN BURNS NEW MEANING ONTO MY SKIN!
I AM CRISP WITH NEWNESS
THE DREAM VOMITS UP THE SLUDGE OF ABANDONMENT
SWIMMING IN THE SLUDGE IS A MCKINSEY CONSULTANT!
SWIMMING IN THE SLUDGE IS ARTHUR BALFOUR!
THEY DROWN
                    I AM THE LOVE OF THE DREAM EMBODIED!
                I WILLINGLY DISSOLVE MY BITTER ATTACHMENTS!
                 THE DREAM IS A FUTURISM OF THE SPIRIT!
                       THE SPIRIT IS AN ORALITY!
                   THE SLUDGE IS A STATE DEPARTMENT!
          MY MEMORY RETURNS ME TO THE GREAT EARTHDREAM!
                  PALESTINE IS A DREAM OF THE FUTURE!
                FUTURE IS A PALESTINE OF THE DREAMING

THE FUTURE CALLS MY SECRET NAME
I HEAP MY HEARTS IN PILES!
THE DREAM OF EARTH REVEALS TO US
THE SONG OF INTIFADA!

                                      THE SMOKE DRIFTS GODWARD
                                  AND MAKES A SHAPE LIKE LEILA
                                        HIJACKING SUN SONG!

                WE MAKE GREEN HEAVEN WITH OUR TONGUES!
                    EARTHDREAM SINGS INTO MY MOUTH
                            PALESTINE IS FUTURE'S NAME!
                            OUR LABOR IS A GODLABOR!
       A SOIL FOR OUR GROWING HURT
             AN ANTIEXODUS OF DIRT
      WE RAMPAGE THROUGH THE AIRWAYS OF
      CAPITAL WE BLOCK ITS BREATH!
                                THE STENOGRAPHER
                            IS EASY TO KILL—AND THEN
                            MY FATHER BREATHES OH:

WE WORK LIKE SEA QUEENS!!!!!

WE'VE GOT BETTE DAVIS EYES!!!

                    WE'RE HALFWAY TO GOOD!!!!!

A DEAD COLONIZER IS WORTH A THOUSAND YEARS

IF YOU WANT TO BE BRUTAL CONSIDER YOUR HANDS

WITHIN MY POCKMARKS I FIND ELEVATOR TO SKY

DON'T LOOK FOR LOVERS (LET THEM LOOK FOR YOU)

THE SWEETNESS OF SPIDERS (YES)

NEVER A CAGED PERSON WITHIN OUR SIGHT!!!

ONTOLOGY < VIBES

ARMPITS > NATIONS

SOMEONE SLEEPS WITH SAND TONIGHT

LET'S HOPE THE SEA GETS HUNGRY

APOCALYPSE IS ONLY PERFUME FOR THE BANKERS

CRUELTY IS A SALTLESS MEAL

YOUR ~~BEAUTY~~ RUBBLE TURNS ME TO ~~RUBBLE~~ BEAUTY

LET'S HOPE THE SEA DEVOURS US
AND FEELS FULL

SPIDERS!!!

ARE WEAVING A SAIL TO GET TO HEAVEN

                                          ARE WEAVING A NET TO CATCH EACH OTHER

ARE WEAVING A PAPER TRAIL TO FOLLOW   + FIND A CEO + EXSANGUINATE THEM

ARE WEAVING A SACK TO HOLD POTATOES

ARE WEAVING SOCKS!

                                    ARE WEAVING A WEB TO CATCH EACH OTHER

ARE WEAVING EACH OTHER

ARE WEAVING A PARACHUTE OF SILENCE

                                      ARE WEAVING US INTO EACH OTHER'S MOUTHS

                        ARE WEAVING A SCARF TO WRAP OUR FACES IN

                              TO HIDE THE PARAMETERS OF OUR FACES

                ARE WEAVING US INTO A NEW KIND OF TENTACLE

                                  A NEW KIND OF LEG

                                                          A NEW KIND OF EYE

                              ECSTATICALLY WEAVING A WAY TO FLY

A WAY TO GO THOUSANDS + THOUSANDS OF MILES + NEVER BE LET DOWN

                              ARE WEAVING A SAIL TO LOVE

                                    + ALSO TO KILL

THE FEAR IS IN YOUR HEART IS IN YOUR BANKS IS IN YOUR EYES IS IN YOUR LAWS IS IN YOUR SHOES IS IN YOUR CLOVES IS IN YOUR DIRT IS IN YOUR BREATH IS IN YOUR CARS IS IN YOUR JAILS IS IN YOUR HEART IS IN YOUR BOOKS IS IN YOUR SALT IS IN YOUR PIPES IS IN YOUR PROSE IS IN YOUR BOLTS IS IN YOUR FOOD IS IN YOUR BEES IS IN YOUR LOVE IS IN YOUR ORE IS IN YOUR LACK IS IN YOUR HEART IS IN YOUR PLANTS IS IN YOUR HEART IS IN YOUR FACTS IS IN YOUR CHILD IS IN YOUR HEART IS IN YOUR HEART IS IN YOUR KNOTS IS IN YOUR HEART IS IN YOUR HEART IS IN YOU!

THE NAME OF THE FEAR IN YOUR HEART IS PALESTINE!

LET IT EAT YOUR SPIRIT WHOLE!

THE FEAR IN YOUR HEART OBLITERATES YOUR ACCUMULATION!

YOU HAVE NOTHING! YOU ARE NOTHING!

YOU MUST ALLOW CONSUMPTION OF YOUR FEELINGS!

THE FEAR IS YANKING YOUR DEATH OUT!

THE FEAR IN YOUR HEART IS A FUTURISM! LOOK!

YOU ARE FINALLY MADE OF DANDELIONS! YOU ARE GLORIOUS! USELESS!

LOOK! YOU ARE BEGINNING TO BE FREE!

AND WHAT IS YOUR NAME?

WHAT THEORY HOLDS THE SCREAM INSIDE?

WHICH SCREAM TELLS YOUR SPIRIT ITS NAME?

WHICH BLOOD MEANING MAKES?

?SING COULD YOU YOU TOLD WHO

WHITHER A FUTURISM OF THE TOURNIQUET?

IS THE STRIP AN ONTOLOGY?

IS THIS GRAVE A RECTUM?

IS THIS A GOOD COLOR ON ME?

?IS FATHER MY WHERE KNOW ANYONE DOES

WHAT IS NOT ENSPIRITED?

?NAME YOUR WAS WHAT

?SCREAM YOUR WAS WHAT

FARGO, WHO WILL HAVE REMEMBERED YOUR NAME?

MIRACLEMAKERS
WE TOUCH HEAVEN WITH OUR TOES
HEAVEN LOOKS LIKE US!

WE BUILD OUR OWN FUTURES
WE BUILD THEM TO LOOK LIKE US

NO SOFT POWER OVER "US"!
RADICALLY WE DEFINE WHAT IT MEANS TO BE "US"
OUR SLINGSHOTS ARE A COLLECTIVISM
OUR FISHNETS ARE A NOSTRADAMUS!

RETURN IS A FUTURE IS A PAST!
THE PAST IS A FUTURE WE RETURN TO!
SUNSPOT TASTERS WE RHIZOME
SCIENCERESISTERS WE HEX THE WORLD

ONLY THE END OF THE WORLD FOR US
ONLY THE BIGGEST "US" WE CAN BUILD

IN THE LAND OF NO STATES I WILL LICK YOUR EYEBALLS!
IN THE SLEEP OF NO DOCUMENTS I WILL KISS YOUR IRIS!

THE SOIL RETAINS ITS IDEOLOGIES
THE SOIL TURNS THEM INTO BATATAS

CITY WALL LEAN AGAINST I STROKE YOUR STUBBLE!
TUNNELWALKERS WE DISSOLVE ANY MILITARY!
AN UNDECLARED END TO ALL DECLARATIONS!

THE SUN HAS SET ON THE BRITISH EMPIRE
ON THE AMERICAN EMPIRE
ON THE EMPIRE OF GOLDMAN SACHS!
ON THE EMPIRE OF MILITARY CONTRACTORS!
ON THE EMPIRE OF EVICTIONENFORCERS!
ON THE EMPIRE OF HUNGERCONSULTANTS!
ON THE EMPIRE OF SECURITIZATION!
ON THE EMPIRE OF POSSIBILITYEATERS!

INSIDE A POEM WE FOUND A TUNNEL
INSIDE THE TUNNEL WE FOUND OURSELVES

WE LIKED OUR TASTE!
WE TASTED OUR COLLECTIVISM!
WE REMEMBERED THE LAND WAS ALREADY A MARXISM!
WE REMEMBERED OUR NAMES AND THE ART OF MAKING NEW ONES!

LAY DOWN YOUR ARMS AND I WILL LAY WITH THEM
MAKE ME THE STRINGS OF A GUTTED PIANO
I WILL WRITHE AND MAKE THE SONG OF OUR ONLY NATION
RETURN IS AN ONTOLOGICAL DANCE STEP!
THE BIRDS ARE TEACHING US TO STAY!
FUTURE IS A DIRTY BATATA

EVERY DAY WE ARE SAYING NO TO THE THINGS THAT KEEP US APART!
EVERY DAY WE ARE SAYING NO TO ENCLOSURE!

EVERY DAY WE ARE CRUISING JERUSALEM!
EVERY DAY JERUSALEM IS CRUISING US BACK!

PALESTINE IS A FUTURISM!
FUTURISM IS AN EXPANSIVENESS OF UNDERSTANDING
FUTURISM IS A DEMOLITION OF MONUMENTS!
FUTURISM A RIOTING CACTUS
PALESTINE A RELATION OF LOVELINESS!

FUTURISM IS A PALESTINE!
PALESTINE IS A SYSTEM OF CARE!
CARE IS A FUTURISM OF HANDS!
FUTURISM IS A PALESTINE!
PALESTINE IS ALREADY HERE!
PALESTINE IS ALREADY EVERY WHERE!

◆
◆
◆

Terror Counter

curves of wanting
You

slush funds

of shame

the air
marshal's suspicious

thigh

my object
of desire, revulsion

alone in bed i receive
a notification

22 dead

64 dead a thousand a
blue surge of wrongness

the size of a meatball o
what an informant my skin

every blush
an admission:

 i wanted to be stripped
searched

touched by a ray

*on the inside
some way*

*they say doesn't hurt
but it does*

RITHA' AL-NAFS

I'll begin with fear (in the pit of my stomach.) A grenade wedged against my waist, though I have no experience in the art of war. I've grappled some with grief. Events overtook me, friends betrayed me.
I was playing, I saw, a losing game.
—Samih al-Qasim, "The Tragedy of Houdini the Miraculous"

The new elegy—from [   ]

Cosmos = an understanding [   ]
Cosmos—composite of [   ]
great chain of being
—from Sirhan Sirhan's diary

Passing Season
May '21

,And who was I calling to? All those days in the month of emerald
        month of my birth, who was it I was beseeching?

And I woke in the sun of yellow silence bootstraps spilling out my mouth

And the dead were amassing beneath me and I was tar in the night

And she sings my life

And on Tuesday I put glue on my fingers and made fingers of glue

And the fist was a small protest of the state

And the protest was a small fist to the mouth of the state

And I felt nothing in the throng of loved people

And sitting on the bench I smoked a cigarette

And I smoked another and another after that and wished my lungs
        would give up and release me into the air

And I smoked again and felt sick and I felt the revolt of shame at its rightness

And the next day there were hundreds murdered by the bombs of the state

And every state is only every other state holding hands crossing a picket line

And I am trying to find the voice of the vulnerable lyric

And she sings my life

And I lowered myself into the tar to feel at last held

And when I woke in the sun of yellow silence I saw a single crow
       an omen of death speaking itself into the air

And I knew then that this emerald month would rhyme with the one three years past
       when the summer's lesson had been again the meaninglessness of my life
       when my birth was counted against the loss sanctioned by the state
       when again I knew I was a breath of God in a world of hurricanes

And I recalled the way time moves like an oil spill oozing every way at once

And the Dulles airport had a smoking lounge for which I was grateful

And the timeline brought more dead into the pile of abandonment

And inside my body was a dark pit of nothingness expanding by minutes

And the days in the stolen desert were stretched thin and sharp

And I could not stop imagining the broken trunk of the van crushing my spine

And it was vivid like the feeling of seeing a body pulled from rubble

And all of my theories of rubble are bile in my throat

And in the sky above the stolen desert I see again a single crow
       tracing itself across the blue like a thread in a shroud of air

And still among the omens I feel the numbness of plastic

And she sings my life it don't

And time hurls my body through its web of string and I was nothing

And I was yearning to be crushed and shame was a bile in my mouth

And the pile only grows despite the agony of my speech acts

And despite the cruelty of my speech acts

And despite the formal refinement of my speech acts

And all of my bonds to my kin begin to break or are revealed to be already broken

And I wanted to die

And I walked down the road from the house whose foundation was genocide

And considered the cars passing by with the eye of requited desire

And she sings my life it don't count

And the earth is reaching to grasp my ankles and shake me to say you
      are a part of this you must be militant in the air

And nothing but a reminder of my ineffectual body

And I want to die

And still I cry only in bursts gone as soon as they came

And I see again a single crow and wonder now
      if I might not be seeing instead a single
      group of crows an omen they say of life

And from Jordan they've broken the fence and started home

And this I crow breathlessly to my father through my crystal screen

And bare chests and unity and the monstrousness of the world which has shaped me

And I am tenseless my skin eaten by the voracity of time

And when I return from the stolen desert I remain shattered

And all of this an incantation to break me down

And the van trunk left me alone and did not fulfill the yawning shame of me

And when I returned it was to news of my queer elder and teacher gone by his hands

And how many punctures of earth will render me

And cigarette after cigarette still the way I keep my eyes open

And when I close them only rubble only phone call only pile

And she sings my life

And I go to Gibran's garden to pray

And I sit on a bench and on it engraved WHEN YOU LOVE YOU SHOULD NOT SAY GOD IS IN MY HEART BUT RATHER I AM IN THE HEART OF GOD

And my prayers are for only for safety only for life

And the air is loud with cicada and wind

And why are these my prayers? And what is it I'm searching for?

And what is it if it never comes?

And she sings my life it don't count for nothing.

And the strangeness of desperate grief, its secret keys

And forgiveness lent to me by an unknown hand

And the corrupted spirit of my life
washes itself in the air
        to stand naked in the wind and to melt into the sun

All these days of apocalypse, if you heard me, it was you

In the voice of my agony I was calling to you

Incantation

Absence makes the heart.
Like water, I learn what shape to take

based on the space I must fill today.
I do not believe in object permanence.

I do not believe that dogs are my best friend.
I do believe in ghosts. I rehearse for the role daily.

On days I feel too solid,
I wear the border around my neck.

This way you do not have to
wonder in which language my blood

accumulates. My vein a cyst filled to the brim.
Like an arcade claw machine, I am far too good

at letting go: the world eats my family and their memory
escapes me. I let it. I have learned grief better

done quick and efficient:
too much of it too often to waste

time. My feet grow three inches into the dirt
everywhere I walk. I am rooted.

What can I say? Years ago, my grandfather dug
his heels in against the settlers. As for me,

I am half meaning. Half vagrant.
I have taken the liberty of stitching

a dotted line into my skin. This way
you do not have to

wonder which crime
you're kissing. I do believe words

emerge from walls, and not the other way
around. I do believe in parallel time.

I believe that in it,
I belong somewhere. In it,

my grandfather and I at this very moment
are comparing shoe sizes.

I kiss his soles and taste a dirt I can name.
I wear my family around my neck,

and the faces become new to me again.
If I am not looking at something it is not

real—this makes me a baby.
This makes me difficult to love.

What can I tell you? The things that made us remake us
again and again. Every day my shape escapes me.

I let it. I believe in rockets. I believe in tunneling
underneath words. I believe that god, too, has feet I can kiss.

What can I say? Years ago, my grandfather looked away
and when he looked back, home was gone.

I am trying to believe that if I do not blink,
if I only keep on looking,

It will stay

Songs of Unnaming

                                         I.

the Grand   Jury repeats and re   alleges
the sweetest thing
in the universe is   an honest person I'm building
                                                   my knowledge and to obtain
                                                                     money and
                                                                       property
from those   mortgage lenders   by means of the upset
                                              everyone has a story I cry
                                                                    every day
I've been praying for all the time   actually sadness inside him at
all
times relevant to this indictment they called it a box but it's basically
              wood and that's why it's called a world
and others known and unknown to the Grand Jury read this to find themselves

in some lines unbelievable   that no one lacks anything for God's sake
life takes from everyone

II.

o God grant us
a relief from the
good tidings we
love
the days that
 ease the
mercies that
continue newly-
built

multi-unit
condominium
properties
material false

and fraudulent
pretenses
representations

and promises
and the
concealment of
material facts
this indictment
building the

bodies
masterpieces in
the company

of honorable
people there is
no power or
strength
fraudulent
scheme in
substance as set
forth

in some lines
love morals and
the best trades
the wellness
that we are
blessed with the
certainty that
relieves hearts

federally
chartered and
insured
depository
institutions

a down
payment credit
from seller to
buyer toys
shoes sun

glasses the days
of adversity and
affliction
Fannie Mae
Form 1003

or Freddie Mac
Form 65 the
attainment of
hope the
pleasure of
forgiveness

it's nothing I
wanted

for us to be
together that
you were here

III.

lender relies on the accuracy of the of I had a great dream a while ago and someone who
cries everyday on people gone from the world and someone suffers from
alienation knowingly and with intent to defraud devised participated in it
paid me almost dirt the destinies of destiny the executor of the
judiciary to pay your salary in the way that pleases me
may God have mercy on every precious soul
under the wealth the various parties to
the transaction together with
others it's nothing I
wanted I didn't
want to
be
away
from you and a
person tired of sacrifice
without results I was trying to
for God's sake and deprivation and loss
employment income assets and liabilities let it
pass on as many times as possible make the end of what
remains of our lives better than what has passed until the rope
stays stretched between you and god knowingly combined conspired and
agreed happiness this is a true bill

IV.

happiness making the bodies
I was average USE OF WIRES
not by marriage nor by children
aided and abetted by others
known and unknown not friends
or travel not with certificates

    or with brands I didn't have time to finish
              I didn't have enough money neither in
   positions nor in welfare neither at homes houses in the states
                      are made of wood if you remember their work is cut off

and we are their hope happiness A TRUE BILL   oh God I remembered them so
                          bless me
with those who remind me   when the reasons are
                            cut off
unfortunately I didn't have a chance happier and worse it was too late just take a deep
breath and say thank God the next one better
     and fear
it affects the heartbeat you were too young o God
       and the time difference by the time they told me water
               every dead person under the dust

                                            with a rain

make it a
year in
which we don't
have a chest this is a prayer
              for our dead

Prayer

       but there was a little girl
       pulled from the rubble

       and there was a cousin
       murdered in the dailiness

       there was a beloved
       pulled into the document

       beyond the poem's groping walls
       outside its foreclosed imaginary

       may they rest

       may we raze the world
       that will not let them

In the Knowledge That You Will Die, and I Will Die
for my baba

                                                      And we will walk

                                                          Into nowhere

                              You with Your smallness and me with my smallness

                                The beach where we froze—were frozen—together

                                      When the patrol officer held You he held You

                                          When You held me You held me   close

                              I answer the video call and Your hair has become white

                                         Thin and vanishing—poverty—wraithlike—

                                                Some incontrovertibility inside of us

                                                       And our times

I answer the video call smoking and You say *You smoke now?* then light up with me

                                         The two of us and our cigarettes and distance

                                                Stumbling along toward death

     When my poems disintegrate You will remain in the documents of the court

          When the courts disintegrate You will slip with me into anonymity

                        Where we began and where we looked for love

The indictment text holding You still and frozen

Where You are defending Yourself against the being-told-of

And You are named Defendant Last Name First Name

And You are named for me and I for You

The pages typed by somebody's hands

Who listened around You shapeless in the clear light

I keep telling You about time

And what we need it for

Though I do not believe—

We find ourselves this morning in our capitols

Farther than a ship from safety

On the horizon line

Its vagueness and its cruelty

I have told Your story and You in Your way

You have told mine

You have told it to me

We tell each other the temperature and find that the numbers match

And I look for You in the white of my own hair

Its unexpected entrances

To miss each other's funerals because of our difference

To have lost, finally, our eachness

To be, finally, no discrete things to be legislated

I wander through the ghosts of Your hair

I wander through what remains of You

In the holding

We are not repeated here

We traverse some space outside of narratability

We are somewhere nobody can see us

And here You tell me I am whole and wholly Yours

And here I tell You I let You go, again and again, each day

And here we are sweetly entangled and disentangling

Somewhere beyond the electronics store and its robberies

Your hair is becoming its own memory of itself

And Your jacket resides on me like a welcome tick

Drawing from me my life

My somewhereness and my penchants-for-

I, begging some God for illegibility

You, forgotten dream of instability

*

Each day You resist my attempts to narrate You

In a manner pleasing to the censors of the spirit

And I learn how to love

What we say to one another becomes electricity

Which in turn becomes speech

I look for You in the wavering frequencies

I look for You in the mistranslated texts

The way Your hand held Me

In the quiet of a rented room

The largeness of the fever's noise

In my ears

A rushing which moved us toward death

And so toward each other

To be or to be always undoing our being

In the hours since I saw You last we have each been lineated

Rain outlining our shapes hapless in the open street

You tell me the house in Jerusalem remains unsold and yet unprofitable

I ask you how your search for work has been

It has not been good

In our electric speech a yearning for unprofitability

That rubble might be our only property

That I might hold Your hand with the same strange force

In Home Depot we built birdhouses

Painted them together and Your breathing soft

You architect of mosques

Forget me and my knife

The sweetness of my living

Your unification

I will forget You

I will forget You and all the houses You did

Or did not build

*

Blue wash faded text trying to write itself across your face

Specter of one way that Marx was fleshly

I wish I knew the ways to being formless

We rend ourselves more than we are rent

Though I do not believe this is true

In the greenery (*the most beautiful kind of greenery is the right kind*

of greenery Sirhan writes)

The greenery of the resort—Sanctuary—Elements—

Hatred envelopes me and I am sent to an office

I have been laced—I smell of anthrax—cumin—

You live in the places I keep You

Paper in a chemical dress rinsed in the grimy sink

The building worth more than our collected organs

The writing (backward) whispers *eating the universe and all humans*

Undried and so unclear illegible a ruin of meaning

I hope You're alright

(*workers of the world unite you have nothing to lose*

but your chains writes Sirhan the last entry in his diary—

they sell a page of it online at Walmart—)

Silence builds upon itself like paper mache

My hands are slick and stuck to a grave that hasn't been dug yet

When I see You again, I wonder where that will be

On the other side of some portal

Through a thicker pane of sorrow

The writing (backward) shouting

The distance is an illusion

All we are is the distance

*

Your birthday on a day I considered dying

As an abstraction

Fireworks encroaching on the boundaries of my shape

Placing me somewhere I am closer to your life

To carve from ourselves at once a meaning and its enemy

You are sung to

I am the song

What petition to save us from the bounds of this world

What change

Fugitives against the text

Bars of white slashed across our eyes

Unknowingness the sign of our tenderness

Our arms casting about for each other in the blue

You in the heat of snow—insidious hope—

I wish my body a handful of the stuff

To drink or nourish some small angel

Tunnels through the regimented words

Definitions of dust—specters in the motes—

I carve You from the blocks

Your image a composite of cosmic dysfunction

Transcendent past the seconds of historiography

I will meet You in the unrubbled home

I will think of Sirhan

Reaching in the well for water and finding a severed hand

Transitory refuge—rupture in earth—hypnotic—

I have realized how much knowledge about myself I lack

I don't know about myself

His handwriting barely decipherable

Built upon itself like ruins of Troy—accretion of rubble—

I ask You what you want

Only to see you habibi

The abscess in my tooth or the dream of my tooth

To have leapt through each apocalypse

From photograph to photograph

Your smile the teeth yellow like mine

In my pocket the whitening strips

This sprawl of language to undo language

My singular rocket—small stone against the text—

Dig your well before you are thirsty writes Sirhan

Desperation his organizing principle

And mine

Wherever You are I reach to You in agony

You reach in Your way

In Your regret

The words a container in which we don't fit

Our cramped togetherness

Our immaterial togetherness

Equality before and <u>after</u> the law

The underline a doorway to unlinearity

Where I will find You

And Sirhan will find us both

Precious only to each other

I am collecting the possibilities

Of stowing myself inside this missive

Of hurling my self toward You

And hurling us both into impermissible vanishing

Life is ambivalence

Life is a struggle

Life is wicked

If life is in any way otherwise I have honestly never seen it

I always seem to be on the losing end

Here on the losing end

We find each other

And like Sirhan we scrawl our names

Over and over until they lose

Any meaning

Dissolved like sugar—sweetness—we shed at last

The illusion of our separateness

*

And I become a breeze

As You have asked of me

And the breeze enters me

The breeze illuminates my sorrow caves

Though I have not yet spoken truly to You

In Your excellent dwelling on the Earth

You have illuminated my sorrow caves

Where You are named noble, of strong passion

I do what I must needs do

To slide with You into our unknowing

Belovedly I pull down our traces

The kindnesses and the mistranslations

The questions asked and unanswered

What intimacy is I do not know

And yet—

Inside of our caves nothing is printed

Nothing remains beyond the knowledge of our spirits

How they do not dance

Nor spurn the Earth

What page to us recalls any thing besides cruelty?

I have made You

I have made You into some language commodity

And I learn each day to release You

You have made Me

You have made Me into some distant flame

And each day You learn to let Me burn

What have we earned in this life aside from quiet

What have we decided we must do

Repair Your heart, Beloved

I will find You again

When I have repaired mine

And we will walk

My hands recalling their terror and forgetting

Your hands recalling their cruelty and forgetting

And no document can keep us now

Not I, with my scrutability finally unnamed

Not You, with Your velocity finally unmoored

You, the song of an animal without a kingdom

You, the last moments of a dying fire

You, the last failure of the court and the extradition

You, applause of a person, emptiness of a person

You, my best and only break

You, toward whom my every performance was aimed and enspirited

Baba, Thou, unloved, unlucky, be loved, be wind, be gone

Language will always be trying to hold You

And i will always be trying

to let you go

◇
◇
◇

Terror Counter

> *everybody loses me. i get lost.*
> *i am loss. a meal for a historical owl.*
> *my bones regurgitated, neatly*
> *piled in the black site of American literature.*
> *i was a we. we were a curse.*
> *panic, debt, the united states district court for the Of,*
> *wood, stone, panic. ours not to ever survive,*
> *ours to be done to and die.*
> *charge of the grand jury.*
> *everything is extant. nothing is extricable.*
> *grief codified like a promissory note.*
> *they have kept me in forms by myself,*
> *huddled against the sharp light of perpetuity.*
> *skin coated with a thinner film of terror.*
> *settling into relations.*
> *half of what i say is meaningless*
> *but i say it so the other half may reach you.*
> *fingertips poking through breaks in the line.*
> *so lonely i miss being surveilled. so desperate i'd count*
> *every fear for You,*
> *sing You to sleep with my hands in*
> *plain sigh. but i. i. i. i. i. i.*
> *i. i. i. i. i. i. i. i. i. i. i. i. i. i. i. i. i. i. i am*

> *a we. we are the dirt.*
> *we tasted the future. You weren't there.*
> *jaws of the world breaking on our tomorrow muscles.*
> *kiss me in language of tunnels we need*
> *exorbitantly we feel*
> *entirely alone*
> *we condemn the recent*
> *we are the recent*
> *cannibalized for tax exempt donations and sonnets*

but tunnel takes me to future
future pries my soul from my teeth
and asks it what my name was
and reminds me when i do not know

and when they come looking for us
god willing we will be some
where else

and at last i will remember

how to forget myself

and in that wail of forgetting

be found

Notes & Acknowledgments

"Passing Season" is in conversation with Iris Dement's song "My Life."

The text in "Songs of Unnaming" is gleaned from interviews with my father, the text of his indictment, and algorithmic mistranslations of his Facebook posts.

In "Terror Counter (everybody…)," the line "half of what I say is meaningless / but I say it so the other half may reach you" comes from Kahlil Gibran's *Sand and Foam*.

Poems in this manuscript have appeared in the following journals, sometimes in earlier versions:

Action Fokus: "Terror Counter (everything is extricable)," "An American Writes a Poem," "Olive Tree Pastoral," "Gazan Tunnel Through Yehuda Amichai's 'Sonnet,'" "Gazan Tunnel through the Balfour Declaration," "PALESTINE IS A FUTURISM: PROPOSITIONS (DIRT IS . . .)," "PALESTINE IS A FUTURISM: WORK (THE FUTURE CALLS . . .)," "Terror Counter ("curves")"

Afternoon Visitor: "Spiders" as "palestinians handshake emoji spiders"

bahr: "PALESTINE IS A FUTURISM (A DEAD COLONIZER…)" as "PALESTINE IS A FUTURISM (NEOLOGISMS)"

Communication and Critical/Cultural Studies: "PALESTINE IS A FUTURISM (MIRACLEMAKERS…)" as "PALESTINE IS A FUTURITY: PROPHECIES (CRUISING JERUSALEM)"

Gulf Coast Journal: "Palestinian Love Poem" (p. 14) and "Palestinian Love Poem" (p. 20)

marlskarx: "For Sami Abu Diak"

Mizna: "Incantation" as "american-Palestinian incantation", "An American Writes a Poem," "PALESTINE IS A FUTURISM (SPIDERS)", "Through USA v Abaji et al"

Nomadic Ground: "Poetry" as "Poetry to a Palestinian"

Poem-A-Day: "The Dream of the Anti-Ekphrasis"

Poetry Daily: "Incantation" as "american-Palestinian incantation"

Prolit: "Parable" as "The Wise American Poet Brings Peace to the Middle East"

Protean Mag: "Of"

Shade Literary Journal: "PALESTINE IS A FUTURISM (EMPTINESSES…)"

Strange Horizons: "PALESTINE IS A FUTURISM (THE DREAM…)"

wildness: "Olive Tree Necropastoral"

This book would not exist without the kindness, feedback, advice, friendship, thought, and care of: Rasha Abdulhadi, George Abraham, Jay Deshpande, Natalie Diaz, Ellie Dries, Hazem Fahmy, Summer Farah, Noor Hindi, Fady Joudah, Mona Kareem, Jess Rizkallah, Solmaz Sharif, Peter Twal.

Thank you to the 2021 Brooklyn Poets Mentorship cohort, the 2020 Tin House Summer Workshop cohort, and everyone I've learned with and from in the writing of this book.

Thank you to my family: Wajieh, Claire, Skaya, Max. May we find liberation within this lifetime, whatever this lifetime turns out to be.

Fargo Nissim Tbakhi is a Palestinian performance artist.

• CENTRAL TRACK POETRY SERIES •

SMU Project Poëtica and Deep Vellum are proud to partner on Central Track, an initiative to publish and promote the art of poetry. Both located in the great poetry hub of Dallas, we share a commitment to support poetry in its various forms and expressions, helping it to flourish locally, nationally, and internationally.

www.ingramcontent.com/pod-product-compliance
Lightning Source LLC
Chambersburg PA
CBHW051511100526
44585CB00043B/2467